Bodyservant

Also by Kit Fryatt

turn push / turn pull
Rain Down Can
The Co. Durham Miner's Granddaughter's Farewell
      to the Harlan County Miner's Grandson.

Kit Fryatt

Bodyservant

Shearsman Books

First published in the United Kingdom in 2018 by
Shearsman Books
50 Westons Hill Drive
Emersons Green
BRISTOL
BS16 7DF

Shearsman Books Ltd Registered Office
30–31 St. James Place, Mangotsfield, Bristol BS16 9JB
(this address not for correspondence)

www.shearsman.com

ISBN 978-1-84861-577-9

ACKNOWLEDGEMENTS
Versions of these poems have appeared in the following anthologies:

Glitter is a Gender, eds Sarah Crewe and Sophie Mayer
(Contraband Books, 2013)

Centrifugal : Contemporary Poetry of Guadalajara and Dublin
ed. Christodoulos Makris and Ángel Ortuño
(EBL-Cielo Abierto / Conaculta, 2014).

Birdbook III, eds Kirsten Irving and Jon Stone (Sidekick Books, 2015)

And in these journals:
Penduline, Dusie, Icarus, Translation Ireland, ESCPoetry.

Contents

bodyservant

I sleep at the foot of the stair
                 the rough nights
                           of the bed
I know his sleeping breath and its feint
                       perhaps he knows mine

his lungs are congested
              he is close to sixty
                   and I am past
                        this year
                           the middle of life

the fair hair he cut   the night before we started
        a four years' pelt   for Cairo
that would not shame the Magdalen
              is gone as he said   a stringy tonsure
                  it would be

when an attack wakes him I bring milk & ale

   we have both killed men that
               he might live to this pass

   their grey shades stand between us
                  so he seems
                      insubstantial

he suffers as tall men do worst with his knees
                  his back
   in the mornings he is agile like an anvil
                as the mounting block he refuses

he and his wife had eleven children
             and some of them live

                                        far away
                                                he misses
her hand beneath his head
                        he says
                                        to put my hand under his head
would be worth the ransom of the son of the king of Cairo
                                        but I've never been lucky

                                        there was a lady
                        the guest of many important men
            he visited her when she stayed with them
then I watched till dawn
                                    I knew her name but never her face
                        she was a grey shape in thought
                            like a place where a painter meant
                        to fill in one of the three Marys

a grey form lying on
                        the body I know better than my own
                                                its scar furrows
                    turn and turn about

the body to which I attribute
                        every scar on my own
                                        lying on a grey form

until I called out
                my fine friend
                    here comes the dawn
                            chief glory
                                glorious lord
                                        here comes the

dawn

Bülbülüm altın kafeste

The prescription is a reed pipe and a
concertina in my pocket, I shred
bus tickets too, paper doilies, all the roses
this year were dipped in glitter, glue
first, the singer's voice fills my head-
phones with Turkish, the empty jute shopper
at my calf has ladybirds on it, must be funny
if your job is dipping Valentine roses
in glue (peculiar), it was supposed to be
Atatürk's favourite song, but I'd say he just
said the first thing that came into his head,
like 'the small town of no importance'
he made his capital. I have to say one thing
this Primark spring range makes modest
dress affordable for once, yay, the lamps they
use to set gel nails might be carcinogenic,
I take out my Galaxy phone in its indigo
rubber skin and think of false nails prodding
touchscreens, crusty with jewels,
these are my friends, but I don't change
the song, which is sad, check messages
or want to go for coffee and cake.
Two kids on BMXs get in my way
he hisses back at his sister, she says
a gaping sorry and so does he,
I smile and say it's all right, I must've been
looking stern, the song is so sad
it's a cliché, but even naïve art
is chock full (especially) of meta
(my love is sick, don't sing)
further up the hill the children pass me
she slouches in the saddle, he stands up
to shout a dare, she hares ahead
their estate tilts, the sky is violet night

the riders of the twilight of this world
sport pennants, decals and spokesters,
alto burrs. The little strip mall is a bizarre
caravanserai. Women's voices break
and they have Adam's apples in fact
the nightingale jars out of a place
railed around and hedged in. It is
goserelin, which looks to me like a Turkish
word—I wonder what the pharmacist
thinks—

I find

I'm on my way to you, tutelar
shabby and locked, if there's single malt
in your nostrils you don't need it
in your mouth
              last time I got laid
someone else's bacon was frying
up the stair combined
with spermicide it smelled like olives
steeping in brine
              I would say Turkey
but others would say Greece
and be no less wrong. One day this whole
mentor/pupil thing will have to end
in the sack
              or throwing delft
but not yet, my good sweet
honey lord, not yet. I want to be
your rawboned hauflin loon
so we can be
              Davy and Alan
staging a bit of hurt/comfort to cadge
a boat, I want to shuck you like an eel,
box you like a hare, put you in my mouth
like a Jew's harp
              I can turn meat to fruit
call it a superpower. You've been
my Hays Code through most of *Twentieth
Century*, one boat-long foot
on the floor at all times
              but in the middle of the bed
the river runs deep, you've managed to
raincheck joy compleat once again forever
I am a narroweyed freightjumping
Appalachian urchin

with tattooed knuckles
a knackered paperback of *A Good Man
Is Hard To Find and Other Stories*
splayed open on my shoulder
bleeding
                  into my panties
as kids have done since before
there were panties and I am riding riding
riding riding riding this boxcar away
from you, tutelar.

Poem beginning with a line by Patrick Califia

I've lost track of how many men I've put my hand into, and it still puts
        me in a trance.

trance body
body loom
bone shuttle
sinew web
weave peace
battle looms

I have lost track of
Wulf   wolf
skin is always touching
the air   almost
so startling   I need
to prove it with a blade.

I will become him
he will take me in.
He clasped me
I entered him.
lodged beneath his ribs
quartered on an island

his skin is always touching iron
it is how he knows
his skin is not always touching earth

last time Wulf
his swordbelt, his brynie
his seax
gift
          my thridings
lay at our feet

I've lost track of how many wolves
I've put my hand into
the king over the gashy fen
exacts tribute of 300 pelts a year

thick throat underfur
fleas spring to the first cut
muscle under its
clear glair veil
against the air,
against the airts
you can never get to them all
before the bellies
green and grey
burst cack
they reek even if you don't
cut the buoyant greygreen bag
someone is always covered in wolfshit
the boy is always waving a wolfprick

I free the hindlegs into meat
press the pads to see the claws flex
different from us

when I crawled inside him
the thumb I use to hold and shear
crined away, and my knee bent backwards
wolfpricks have a bone
baculum
unlike ourselves

I roar at the boy to stop messing
tempted to toy
with the tail myself: bonewhip thrash

last time, Wulf
I laughed at you bent over

wriggling out of your mail
           Wulf
you straightened panting hard
Wulf   wolf

his swordbelt, his brynie
his seax
tribute
                  my thridings
lay at our knees

if he comes armed he will be a gift
to the four airts
battle looms

put down that dirty thing you gowk
I collar the boy
knock the pizzle out of his hand
get over here and help
Earl Isengrim out of his coat
the head is tricky
the inside out guessing
it takes to find eye and lip
there's no muscle
here no fat
half the time I don't
get the snout quite right
I hold it up raw side out
lunge and wrap the boy in it
he shrieks and struggles

I release him, he's laughing, but he says
you cunt, he's clabbered like a new bairn.
If they knew what I was thinking
they'd have me sectioned.

last time Wulf
his swordbelt, his brynie

his seax
need
                my thridings
lay at our heads

the carcass looks
silly clemmed
like the pelt never
was together with it

it takes the two of us
me and the boy
to haul it out to the hounds
it is heavier than either of us
they'd have you sectioned too
there is a skinned wolf
beneath my ribs
if he comes armed
they will quarter him
battle looms

we are different
unlike ourselves
ungelic is us

my body is a loom
shuttle of bone
web of sinew
of sinew and bone
I must weave a peace.

Splice

I said, I don't think it's very noble
but it's a thing a lot of men have done
and more women than you might think
one way or the other, I'm not sure I haven't
done it myself, especially in the way I think
you mean, he looked all who said anything
about and I looked back it's too late to
row back now, remember the photographs
you sent me of your cubby cell
(no shower curtain, it looked oddly sinister)
in that pitted 30s block near the beach
westernised yet vernacular, minor
in its way maybe but fine nonetheless
they're going to knock it down, have knocked
by now I expect, vandalism, it's a lot to
communicate in a look, true, so I said
it doesn't make any difference to how
I feel, I wanted to add, do you expect
me to leave your arms and run shrieking
holy & meek into the West Kerry dunes,
I who have only just got into your arms
and have no hope after this night
of getting into anything else except
bother and certainly never your arms again?

although it almost couldn't be more different
it almost couldn't be more the same, this
bothy with only one internal door, I admire
the consistency of your taste across
thousands of miles and at the same time
reflect how often desire has stranded me
on the wrong side of everything ever,
identifying with power, violence and men,
while you cook, gently submitting

I should read a novel by a woman I've
never heard of, an architect, but this
admission is crafty, it means that if I am
the feminist I claim to be, I should reject you,
save you the embarrassment of rejecting me,
I don't of course oblige, the omelette is
delicious, my feminism is a sham, the novel
evokes the processes of idle fantasy, I am ungentle
for putting you through this, I realise I have not
said anything for a long time in direct
speech here, but *ogni penserio vola*,

in real time I'd only fallen silent for a moment
he nuzzled my hair, I strove with my woman's
voice to speak big, to say something
fierce, loyal and chivalrous, forgetting
that other people do not share my fealty-kink
and o god no, he said, I don't want you
to abase yourself, whatever gave you that
idea? it's you, I felt like saying, who is using
this notion of sexual contamination
(forgive me, my demographic is that slim
one all overshadowed by no respecter
of persons, alarmed by present
complacency, regular sexual health checks
should be part of your life, it hasn't
gone away you know) presenting yourself
as damaged goods, to let me down gently,

no, I didn't think that unworthiness till later,
what I remember is reluctance to believe
he did not want my caresses, I prolonged
them, making insincere offers to stop
at his word, after he stiffened, sat up,
drew back, I make nothing of inclinations,
there is an oratory on a shore, there is
a wood on the downs, for god's sake let us

sit upon the ground, *foid far ndís innocht, &*
téit léignid becc etraib co ná dernaid aneaspa,
and we did, no need of little scholar
nor bolster to this bundling, I dreamed

you relented with open-mouthed
kisses on my neck, I had not even dared
try to kiss you, but I still wonder what
separated my conduct from sexual assault,
feminine prerogative? nothing? a Rizla?
woke to the dawn chorus, pointless Silenus
startled by, hell, y^r lack-looks, y^r Angevin
colouring, emotional and credulous dreaming

cognition trying to make sense of real
world stolidity, prickly with humiliation,
Dycun, slepe sicury quile we wake,
and drede nouzt quile we lyve sestow.

on the warren, in the lee of the firs

The west is molten and the east is wrought
iron. Light gropes across the field below the railway
line, the air hums sepia and the wires
are still. A boy is whistling for his dog between
snatches of 'Gil Morrice', or 'Clerk Colville'.

His father comes by and hands him
a briarwood pipe, his nails worry a crack
that springs a thorn. Later he will say
a splinter gashed his thumb, calling
to mind the green, the unbred breed of it.

His mother comes by and hands him
an egg. He cracks it with his nail.
Under the membrane is a catacomb
of dry, entire bones. Later he will say
he misremembers, it was an owl's pellet.

His sister comes by and plucks
her a cherry from a low bough. His teeth
meet no stone but sourness, the tough
membrane of a wet petal. Later he will
say often fruit rots before it is ripe.

His true love comes by and plucks
a quiver from a silver arrow, shows
a shaggy foot. Later he will say
the light moved like shadows and the air was thick
with something. The dog growls and shies.

He has never wondered why.

tardy steps her silent main

going back, when I think back on it she was just
another mould to me—Edward Loughman

It is all quite like the end of the movie
or its pre-credit sequence, a catering forklift
yelping steadily, newes, newes schall rise
shrewstail rain scatting the glass, eh,
the cheap cinema of outside the train,
those people, their poignant dwelling
in routine and soft white lamplight
relief, sink into the major-key motif swelling
over brushed drums and plucked bass,
now it is vain so now it is vain so
for the sight of a plaster figurine
transfixes and sobs the breath out of me
for cowardice, for love refused.

The hermit and the crow

Royston, 154-

In winter the crows fly south to eat mutton, the ravenous mutton
that puts men on the road. Halfway down my road
I entered a cave and saw no crows for thirty years.

A man cannot eat a pension, he must like archbishops
and swords eat meat, or perhaps he can eat crow.
I am put on the road by men, not fleeces.

Tomorrow my home will be a hole in the ground, that eats earth
like princes, saints and horses, like the child himself
who, crowing, rode the giant's shoulder.

I will hood my eyes so as to taste the air, crows will bring me bread
but it will be the bread of crows (that aids sight, because
first crows pluck the eye) not the broken bread of men.

The crow's feathers are grey, St Lawrence's greasy charnel,
I am done to a turn, take a bite. Her hood is as Katharine's,
that all the fine ladies wore when last I saw a crow.

She fears no cuckoo and is friend to the stork. She follows
her son as an escort, as Empress Helena brought the rood
in her beak, and her croak bespeaks rain.

David's topknot tilts, he snaps stubby wingtips, wheeling
before the kist until his glossy shanks are black. His wife
beats the stuffing out of him, the sheepish, the broken roué.

It is very wicked to believe that God tells his secrets to crows,
but who, having seen their kindliness, their span soar rude
over crow-grey scrub, would doubt that God is a crow, and his mother?

I lived alone for thirty years, and hoped to die before I was lonely
put out on the roads of men. What may I do but trust hugger-mugger
in the half-solitariness of crows, that they shall have my heart?

Fulminate

after Catullus, Carmen 16

I'll fuck you both and fuck your fucking faces
Aurelius, you nonce, you bitch Furius
who think I must be some kind of pussy creep
because my verse is tender, mildly risqué.
A poet should be well-mannered and decent
the poetry itself, not so much, maybe,
the which (mine, anyway) has a grain of wit
because it's tender, a little bit risqué
enough to rouse an itch and scratch it, not just
in spotty kids, but in hairy old geezers
who otherwise couldn't get it up at all.
You read about my thousand kisses and now
you fucks think a kisser hasn't got a cock?
Fuck you fuckers and fuck your fucking faces.

Saffron Laudanum

I counterfeit sleep but my flinch when a cup
in your claw bends and levels with me is real.
The best ceps grow on the north side of the churchyard,
you got the settee I've slept on these last nights
in a catacomb. I'm settling to the new currency
of our friendship, but everything I say comes out
tinny and clipped, too much small change. John Newman
was burned here in the square, in 1555, your sitting room
is freezing. That was for heresy, under Mary,
but counterfeiters—if they were women—also burned.

Mine owne Ned Poins, dark pool
liquidity reflects the terminal frequency
of greenscreen, it's picking up along
the river and my scalp stings where
it's shaved to the eartips, if I hadn't
left my Monmouth cap in that condensation-
sodden crank food café I'd put it on
and my collar up against the electric bray
of thirty thousand chartered dolts,
each with a sprig of paper skagbloom
in his coat, the more jerk that
it's not the sort of pap that feeds
a dream on, sometimes you feel
you're going against the grain
just to hold the camber of the road.
I think, I'm out of work, back home
there's a cup of warm piss a berserker
left on the windowsill and this
city's a good one to fly, or swim in.

My Poins, I cannot thread a dromedary
through echo charlie two romeo but then
again, I can't not, green light plays
on a lake of tryacle, we are in thrall
to all the goliath trixies ever laid by flow
traders in an antic time; in echo eight
drivers the enlarged posterior hippocampus
is a result of the knowledge base to echo
charlie three mike (thine owne)
the gold-plated wildmare rarees out
of a turbo carapace, the photocopier
lamp passes hot and green under
my palm, the marine cavalier braces
his golden thighs to hold the cant
of the shell, the faithful reprobate
writes so to his bean manly alice oh!

Dolly dorcas to all comers, dowriest cod
on herself, naff brute that in utter scharda
zhooshes their martinis with her own flayed pelt
pupped to cark, no pity, ducky & no praise.
I'd do the very same for my bean butch affair
zhooshing his skin with my nantizhoosh stiff,
like a snake that drops its schmutter
by carking it to become not so.
If only my pelt was all over bona riah
to reef his, to park him such fantabulosa drag
that would fairly charver his filly lucoddy
his box, his cavalier bagadja, bold as day,
ducky, even to be the batts that plate his lyles,
so he could troll and mince all over me for a year or two.

We have not yet done as we ought
and shall we swing for it, hard choad,
my Poins, judge me how I spend
even into that scuzzy intercrural gap
that were thy peach colourd once
green digits spill through the blind slats
onto your cheeks, scroll up your spine;
here we are, my shadow, just come
at cockcrow in Kent and Christendom
(gently rise and do not even softly call)
you vanishing, and I answer: *dead elm.*

Hero

Across the stream a man is standing.
I want him. I want his body. If you understand
the difference, I don't. He's dressed for three-
quarters of a century ago, decent déshabillé:
barefoot, thin worsted trousers, shirt untucked
and open. His back is to me, he's facing away,
did I say that? One hip thrust out with all
the fragile self-esteem of those gay old photographs
and under rationed flannels his belly,
taut and convex, forms a funnel—part of my brain
reels away and thinks of Lower Drumcondra
I have worked in Lower Drumcondra for the best part
of a decade and the worst best part of my life
and I have never heard anyone say *tundish*
forgive me, it's just the way I'm made—
of muscle, and his cock's the spout of it. Rilke
called it a smile, and it does occur in nature, rarely,
rarely. I will him to strip (and he does!) so I may
take in his rangy shoulders, the breathtaking
incurve above that almost-articulate arse, lean thighs
and furzy calves, so I can see what awaits me,
cracked hard skin on the heel, the other foot
unseen in the long grass. What will he say,
when he turns his head, showing me my face
in a horn-backed mirror, what will he say, in my chest
voice, the voice I keep locked away, the voice
in my head, my buzzing brainpan, will he say
the water is wide, I cannot swim over (to which
I make *replie, you are deceaved, I am no woman
I*) or lift his hidden hoof and say *these are the hills
of heaven, my dear, where you shall never win*?

IOU | OUI

the prayer

oh She!

alpha better omega

Black woman
because black is the colour
of my true love's

locks

set free with a bound

auntie norn
three eye testifier

whose earrings are manchild corpses

who

childlike and unperturbed
is very dear to her

cuntstruck
top tits: long shelf life
snarl: the void

what big teeth you have
and a tongue all the better to lick

out

her skull-goblet
meus inebrians
skull-ruff: alphabet

whose two right hands make the signs of danger and desire
that is one sign
whose upper left hand holds a sword
whose nether left hand holds a head

because she is her own perseus

sky-clad spacecadet

naked and unperturbed

a chatelaine of severed hands
because hands are karma
because hands that do dishes

because she blissfully fucks a corpse

undead
cums in the charnel yard

becomes the charnel yard
the charnel yard becomes her

her patteren
ring flowerengine fivefortress

gross and subtle

pleasurelease

boon fruits

forgiveusoutrespasses

oh Hymn!

forgive my kidding around
give me luck
guard my life
high honour
guard my girl
my boys
my bread

please release me
let me go

i am your arthur i am your arthuress you are my avalon

1.

oh You!

joke caster
motherwife
who laid low
three cities

ok caste

this is poetry
streaming from my gob like blood
thunderwoman

i am your arthur i am your arthuress you are my avalon

2.

oh You!

dangly earring girl
whose earrings are boy bodies
whose earrings are punk spunk
whose earrings are arrows

(oh my very dear)

cum into the mouth of speech
cum into my mouth the argos-eyed
votary of the argos jewellery counter

i am your arthur i am your arthuress you are my avalon

3.
Oh You!

lockslady all
blood streaming from your gob like poetry
who laid low three earths

i am your arthur i am your arthuress you are my avalon

4.

oh You!

miss sharp
bite my head off wont ya
up yours

(*the gesture which dispels fear*)

gimme gimme
what i want
booty

i am your arthur i am your arthuress you are my avalon

5.

Oh You!

do

the ooh
lip
oh

and become a lovegodsgift

i am your arthur i am your arthuress you are my avalon

6.

oh You!

gold-top tits
skull ruff
give me wood
cum into the mouth of speech

i am your arthur i am your arthuress you are my avalon

7.

oh You!

when i think on you
space cladette
three-eyed testifier
chatelaine of severed arms
corpse-fucker
cemetery zombie

doesn't make me a poet, does it?
(maybe it does)

i am your arthur i am your arthuress you are my avalon

8.

oh You!

girl i'm crushing on
girl i'm crushing hard for
let's go drinking in the cemetery
diamond white and twenty twenty
ten lambert & butler

you'll gape puking
i'll hold your hair
i'll still kiss you afterwards
hyena hungry
like a drain

i am your arthur i am your arthuress you are my avalon

9.

oh You!

i'm pigthick as shit
i can't even

don't get cross honey

i am your arthur i am your arthuress you are my avalon

10.

oh You!

if i think of you alone in my room at night and i'm naked and my hair's a locked nest with american crew and my hands are idle if i think of you then

so what?

i am your arthur i am your arthuress you are my avalon

11.

oh You!

i'm going to repeat myself
i'm going to repeat myself

i'm going to repeat myself

I'm not

almighty wise

i am your arthur i am your arthuress you are my avalon

12.

oh My!

you my ever thing
babe
i think some time the hole world
must cum out yr cunt

i am your arthur i am your arthuress you are my avalon

13.

oh You!

some people don't adore you
they're wrong
alpha girl
gods adore you devils adore you

i am your arthur i am your arthuress you are my avalon

14.

oh You!

mercy mercy me
lady
let me sink in you
or just burn
my boats
not sleeping
but dead

i am not your arthur i am not your arthuress you are still my avalon

15.

oh You!

if i think on you in the cemetery in the nip and cum on a thousand
flowers

does that make me?

i am your arthur i am your arthuress you are my avalon

16.

oh You!

if i think on you on a tuesday when i'm alone mooching round the
cemetery smoking or when i razor my sides and slick up my hawk with
sugar water i might just cum on the ground if i think of you then

so what
doesn't make me a poet does it?
is there an elephant in this

skiff

i am your arthur i am your arthuress you are my avalon

17.

oh You!

if i fill your cranny with petals
if i repeat myself
if i fill your cranny with petals
if I repeat myself
if I fill your petals with wood
if I repeat myself
if I fill your petals with wood

rough
that's poetry
that is
gallons of nectar
if I fill your petals with blood

i'll take ship on it

not sleeping
dead

i am your arthur i am your arthuress you are my avalon

18.

oh You!

if i think of your smile when my hands are idle it turns into one of
those corpse-fucking skull-fucking trances

not sleeping
dead
drowning
burn my boats

i am your arthur i am your arthuress you are my avalon

19.

oh You!

my ever thing
becomes the accomplishment

because i adore your meat
jump your bones

a ruff of bright wood

my gift to you

& cats & camels & sheep & buffaloes & elephants

& men

i am your arthur i am your arthuress you are my avalon

20.

oh You!

if i hold back
deeply enlisted in your cunt
if i'm naked in my room at night
in sweet amorous play with my girl

lotusing on your feet

so what?

i am your arthur i am your arthuress you are my avalon

21.

oh You!

i celebrate yourself and sing yourself
i lean and lotus at my ease
who holds you now in hand

or foot

becomes large

i am your arthur i am your arthuress you are my avalon

22.

oh You!

the world is full of deer girls with animé eyes
and i could have any of them
drag kings
to my cell block ache
total ecstasy

locked

i've drowned my boats
not sleeping
dead

i am your arthur i am your arthuress you are my avalon

the obeisance

oh You!

saviour & someone's wife
on my knees for you
on my face

i am your arthur i am your arthuress you are my avalon

the colophon

oh Hymn!

true mirror of my dangly earring girl
arthur arthuress
traitor translator
total ecstasy votary
taste her tang
in your throat

in

say *culo* say *culo* o ram

yeah

Pros of the Transsiberian & little Flint of the Ronson

for the unsung

Back then I was in my teens (nor am I out of them)
barely 500 years dead and I wouldn't remember my childhood
if you paid me, and though (*pace* little Flint) I don't think
you can be 16.000 leagues from anywhere on the face of the earth
I was a tidy steppe from my birthplace
I was in Moscow,
city of one thousand and three campaniles and 7 railway stations
and I hadn't got enough already of the 1003 campaniles and seven
        railway stations
because my flaming adolescence was such a drag
that my heart was burning, turn and turnabout, like the Temple of Artemis
with a herostratic love, or like Red Square in Moscow
when the sun goes down.
My eyes were lighting out down those old roads
and I was such a crappy muse
I didn't even know how to get myself there.

The Kremlin was like a huge cake with royal icing
crusted with gold hundreds and thousands,
with the blanched almonds of cathedrals
and the honey gold of bells.
An old nun was telling me tales of Baba Yaga,
I was dry and decrypting Linear A
when the Pentecostal pigeons flocked over the square
and my hands flew up alongside, with the bruising whizz
of an albatross
and these are my last memories of the last day
of the very last journey
and of the sea.

Nonetheless, I was such a shitty muse
I didn't even know how to get myself there.
I was hollow

and all the days and all the fellows in the cafés and glass upon glass
I wanted to take them and break them
and the shopfronts and the streets
and all the houses and the lives
and the wheels of the hackneys raising tornadoes over the potholes
I wanted to shovel them into a blacksmith's forge
I wanted to grind their bones
and rip out their tongues
liquidate their sublime bodies, strange & naked under maddening clothes…
I have seen the coming of the terrible red Christ of the Russian Revolution
and the sun was a hideous lesion
spitting and splitting like firesteel.

Back then I was in my teens (nor am I out of them)
and I still didn't remember nothing about my birthplace already
I was in Moscow, wanting to be a fire-eater
and I couldn't get enough of the towers and the stations, rubbing against
        a *flinty substance*
that formed a *constellation of sparks* in my eyes
sufficient to light an acetylene lamp in the wildest wind.

In Siberia the artillery hammered – it was war.
Hunger cold disease cholera
And the turbid water of Heilong Jiang was bearing its freight of human
        carrion
In the stations I saw the last trains leave,
no-one could leave because there were no more tickets for sale
and the soldiers who were leaving would rather have stayed.
An old nun sang to me: I smell the blood of Russia, the Russian smell.

And I, the worst muse, who didn't want to go anywhere specially, could've
        gone anywhere.
And of course the *entrepreneurs* still had plenty of cash
to make their fortunes with.
Their train left every Friday morning.
There was talk of a lot of deaths.
Someone brought a hundred cases of alarm-clocks and Black Forest
        cuckoo clocks

someone else, hatboxes and stovepipes and corkscrews of Sheffield steel
someone else, coffins from Malmö full of jam and sardines
Then there were a lot of women
touting their thigh-gaps
which (said Flint) would also service
or serve as, I didn't quite catch it,
coffins
but they all had license to trade
there was talk of a lot of deaths out there
they rode concession rate
and even had current accounts.

Now, one morning it was little Flint's turn
It was in December
I left too, keeping company with a traveller in jewellery on his way to
        Harbin
We had two coupes in the express and 34 caskets of jewellery from
        Pforzheim
German carbuncles, made in Germany
He'd got Flint all togged out in new clobber but getting on the train he
        lost a button
I remember I remember but I think sometimes Flint forgets
that we were just a pair of catamites to a travelling tatmonger
and if anything it was me who got him the gig.
We slept on the caskets and I was on top of the world, playing with the
        Ronson Pist-o-Liter
the old fruit had given me
(Flint had a nickel-plated Browning)

We were happy and carefree
We made believe we were bandits
We had stolen the treasure of Golkonda
and by the grace of God and the Transsiberian railway, were going to
        hide it on the other side of the world
Flint defended the loot while
I was the robbers coming down from the Urals to attack the mountebanks
        in Jules Verne

I was the Honghuzi, the Chinese Boxers
and furious Mongolian horsemen
and the Forty Thieves
and the henchmen of the terrible Old Man of the Mountain
and, most modern of all
Raffles and Bunny
and all those international men of mystery.

And yet, and yet
Flint was sad, crying like a baby
The rhythms of the train
The American headshrinkers, they have this thing they call railroad
        neurasthenia:
the doors banging, voices and axle-grinding on the frozen track
the golden filament of futurity
his Browning and the piano and the oaths of the oafs playing cards next
        door
the underwhelming presence of Little Flint
the man in the tinted spectacles who nervously prowled the corridor and
        looked in at him
missing a trick
ladies zhooshing about
the steam whistle
and the perpetual din of the wheels tumbling along a wild and groovy sky
windows iced up
à rebours!
Behind, the Siberian plains, the low sky and the massive umbrage of
        silence, up and down.

Little Flint in his plaid
parti-coloured like his life
which has kept him no warmer than that Caledonian rug
(I'll shelter thee, I'll shelter thee)
the whole of Europe seen through the windcheater
that is an express going full steam ahead
is no richer than my life my poor life
this rug

raveling out on these caskets full of gold
we roll along with them
as we dream
as we smoke
and the only glimmer in the universe
is a poor thought…

I just about laugh myself to mortal tears
if I think, oh Lord of Love, of my mate
he's just a kid, who I found
pale, virginal and spotty, out back of the knocking-shop
where I, assistant deputy bottlewasher-in-chief
was stacking crates
and he came cooling his cold feet.
I had a couple of chits in my arse pocket,
messages to buy and deliver
and I said come along for the ride.

He's only a ginger kid, never laughs,
is sad, smiles, cries way too much.
There's something in his eyes, though,
the poignant heraldic spike of the fleur de lys
call it the yellow flag of his disposition,
or of France.

He's rude and noisy and full of complaint
he'd tempt the tried patience of a goddamn saint
any road along
we wore out a lot of shoeleather that evening
and somehow wound up in the Metropol
courtesy of our patron,
the seller of currency,
I fucked Flint up the arse
he gave me head
and the merchant turned on
us a glittering raisin-black eye.
It was Flint he really wanted

he bought him a new suit and a revolver
and all I got was a novelty lighter
but I said we came as a pair
because we did
(spectacularly)
because what harm can come to two of you?
because despite it all, he's my darling
all other guys seem to come wrapped in leopardskin
and barbells
my poor imp is so lonely, so naked
that when I grip his hips and give it to him
his midriff melts
it's like he has no body at all, he can't afford one.

He's just a spark in charcloth,
the fleur de lys, with its poignant heraldic spike
cold and lonely, the bloom already going off
I could laugh myself to tears thinking of his heart.

Anyway, I just wanted to set that straight
because when Flint tells it it gets maudlin.

And this night is just like a thousand others, a train weaving through it
big star falling
and a pair of lost boys, even if one of them is a girl, love to make love.

The sky is like the tattered canvas of a twopenny ha'penny big top in a
        fishing village
in Flanders
the sun is a smoky lamp
and up on the flying trapeze, in the shape of a moon, is a woman.
The hautboy, sackbut, the reedy flute and broken tabor
and here is my cradle
my cradle
it was always by the pianola, when my mother, like Clive Durham, fed
        Tchaikovsky into it
I spent my childhood in the Temple of Artemis

and the School of Life, behind the trains pulling out of the station
now I pull the trains behind me
Basel-Timbuktu
I've had a flutter at Ascot and Longchamps
Paris-New York
Now the trains run in harness with my life
Madrid-Stockholm
and I've lost all those Super Yankees
There's nothing for it but Patagonia, Patagonia can ease my vast melancholy,
        Patagonia and a South Sea voyage
I am on my way
I am always on my way
I'm on my way with little Flint of the Ronson.

The train takes one gigantic bound and lands on its treads.
The train lands on its treads.
The train always lands on its treads.

'I say, Flint,' I say (it's our little joke) 'are we there yet?'

'You're a long way from Montmartre,' he says, 'you've been trundling
        along for seven days,
'far from the Butte, that brought you up by hand, from the bosom of
        Sacré Coeur
'that you nuzzled
'Paris has gone up in a huge conflagration
'there are just flinders falling back
'the rain falling
'the turf bulging
'Siberia turning, turning,
'Heavy snowdrifts piling,
'the chimes of madness trembling like one last desire in the grey-blue air
'the train pounding in the heart of the leaden horizon
'and your misery chuckles…'

'I say, Flint,' I say (it's our little joke) 'are we there yet?'

'Worries,
'Forget your worries
'All the peeling, carious stations along the way,
'the telegraph wires they dangle from,
'the poles that gesture as if to strangle them
'the world stretches out, elongates like a concertina
'like the lonesome whistle of a blues harp
'tormented by a sadistic hand,
'through rents in the sky, fierce engines
'flee
'the whirling wheels the mouths the voices
'hellhounds on our trail
'the demons are let slip
'any old iron
'everything's a false accord
'the yaketty-yak of the wheels 'shocks
'rebounds
'we're a tempest in a deaf skull…'

'I say, Flint,' I say (it's our little joke) 'are we there yet?'

'Yeah right, you're wearing me down and out, you know full well we're
           far out and in deep

'sweltering madness brangling in the engine
'plague and cholera rise like burning brands around us
'we're heading into war like it's a tunnel, uh-huh, going through the
           tunnel of war
'Famine, that bitch, snatches at routed clouds
'and shits rotting corpses on the battlefield
'do as she does, get to it…'

(I love him when he talks smack like that, he thinks it's smart, OK?)

'I say, Flint,' I say (it's our little joke) 'are we there yet?'

'Yes we are we fucking are
'all the scapegoats have crashed out in the desert
'can you hear the bells on this scabby lot, more cowbell
'Tomsk, Chelyabinsk, Kainsk, river Obi, Taïchet, Verkné-Oudinsk, a lych-
       barrow, Samara, the dreaming cloudcapped spires of K'un Lun…
'Death in Manchuria
'is our destination and last resort
'this is a bad trip
'yesterday morning
'Lucky's hair turned white, (most simple and most ordinary and therefore
       most terrible)
'and Kolya Nicolaï Ivanovitch has been biting his nails to the quick for a
       fortnight
'do as Death and Famine do, get to it
'if it costs a tanner, on the Transiberian it costs a tenner
'set the seats on fire and hide your blush under a bushel
'Old Nick's on the old joanna,
'his gnarly fingering gets the old dears going
'Nature
'hey Fanny
'get to it
'till we get to Harbin…'

'I say, Flint,' I say (it's our little joke) 'are we there yet?'

'No, give me rest, leave me alone…
'Your hipbones jut
'your stomach's upset and you're gone with the gonny
'that's what Paris dropped into your lap
'you got a bit of soul, because you're unhappy
'I'm sorry, sorry for you, come here to me, let me clasp you to my heart
'the wheels are windmills in the land of makebelieve
'and the windmills are a beggar's whirling crutches
'we're legless in space
'we trundle on our four stumps
'our wings have been clipped
'the wings of our cardinal sins

'and all trains are the devil's playthings
'coop, coop
'the modern world
'speed gets you nowhere
'the modern world
'distances are all too distant
'at the end of the road it's terrible to be a man with a woman.'

(Lucky he's not, then, isn't it?)

'I say, Flint,' I say for the last time (it's our little joke) 'are we far from
        Montmartre?'

'I'm sorry, sorry for you, come here close to me I'm going to tell you a story
'Come into my bed,
'let me clasp you to my heart
'I'm going to tell you a story
'Oh come, come!'

'In Fiji spring springs eternally,
'languor,
'lovers swoon in the tall grass and burning pox lurks among the banana trees
'come to the lost isles of the Pacific
'they have names like Phoenix, the Marquesas
'Borneo and Java
'and Celebes, shaped like an elephant.'

'We can't go to Japan
'Come to Mexico
'on the high plateaux tulips bloom
'the creeping lianas are the sun's elaborate coiffure
'it's like a painter's palette and brushes
'colours as noisy as a gong
'Rousseau was here,' (he wasn't)
'and it marked him for life
'it is a land of birds
'the bird of paradise, the lyre bird

'the toucan, the mocking bird
'and the hummingbird nesting in the heart of a black lily
'we'll make love in the magnificent ruins of an Aztec temple
'you'll be my idol
'a gaudy, infantile idol, a bit ugly and bizarrely strange
'Come!'

'If you like we'll get in an aeroplane and fly over the land of a thousand lakes
'nights there are long beyond measure
'our prehistoric ancestors will be scared of the engine noise
'and I'll build a hangar for my plane with mammoth fossils
'the pristine fire will rekindle our poor love
'a samovar
'and we'll make fine suburban love at the Pole,
Oh come!'

'Jeanne Jeannette Ninette ninny baby-blanky booby
'me oh my mama namby-pamby my Newfoundland
'dodo jumbo
'dooby-doo poop
'little cabbage-face
'cocoon
'cutie kiddo 'naughty peachy
sweet treat
'choo-choo
'kitey-kite'

(He's an embarrassment. I pretend to be asleep.)

I pretend to be asleep (and dream)
all this time, I've had to accept so much without question
all those faces glimpsed in stations
all the clocks
Paris time, Berlin time, Saint Petersburg time, railway time
and at Ufa the gunner's face running blood
and the ridiculously bright clockface at Grodno
and the perpetual motion of the train

every morning you put your watch forward
the train advances and the sun retreats
nothing to be done, I hear the bells
the great tocsin of Notre Dame
the shrill bell at the Louvre that rang on St Bartholomew's Day
the rusty bell of Bruges, Life-in-Death
the electric alarums of the the New York Public Library
the campaniles of Venice
and the bells of Moscow, the clock at Red Gate that I clockwatched
when I was in the office
And my memories
the train rumbles over points
the train trundles on
and the gramophone stutters over a Romani march
and the world, like the clock in the Jewish Quarter of Prague, runs crazily
        backwards…

Fling love-me-nots to the wind
here, the storm unloosed
trains roar like cyclones down tortuous tracks
devilish toys
there are trains that never meet
some just get lost along the way
the stationmasters play chess
backgammon
billiards
carom shots
putting English on the ball
the railroad is a new branch of geometry
Syracuse
Archimedes
and the soldier who gutted him
and the galleys
and the destroyers
and the amazing machines he invented
and all that carnage
ancient history

modern history
the whirlwhinds
the shipwrecks
like the Titanic that I read about in the paper
so many associations of ideas that I can't make anything of
because I'm a really shitty muse
because I forgot to take out travel insurance
I don't even know how to get myself there
and I'm scared.

I'm scared
I don't even know how to get myself there
I should do a series of deranged paintings, like Flint's mate Chagall
But I didn't take notes as we went along
Excuse my ignorance
Excuse me for not knowing how to play up and play the poetry game
as Flint's pal Guillaume Apollinaire says
you can learn all you need to know about war from Kropotin's *Memoirs*
or in the bloodthirsty Japanese illustrated papers
but why should I footnote it all?
I give myself up
to the acrobatics of memory…

Around Irkutsk things got slow
started to drag
we were the first to negotiate Lake Baikal
and the train was decked with flags and lanterns
and we'd departed the station to the strains of God Save the Tsar
or Glinka's 'Glory', I didn't know which and Flint said both were
        melancholic
though I couldn't see it myself. If I were a painter I'd
slap on loads of red and yellow because I think we were all a bit mental
and a vast giddiness put blood into the passengers' pinched cheeks.
As we got nearer to Mongolia
that burned like a housefire
the train's allure had gone into definite rallentando
and I sensed in the constant grinding of the wheels

the bloody uncontrolled sobbing
of an eternal liturgy.

I saw.
I saw the dark trains the silent trains the ghost trains coming back from
     the Far East
and my eyes are the lights they had on behind
at Talga 100.000 casualties agonised and none to help
I went to the hospitals in Krasnoyarsk
and near Khilok our paths crossed a line of mad soldiers
and in the quarantine wards I saw oozing sores and gashy wounds and
     exposed organs
and the amputated limbs did a jig or took flight in the savage air
every face was a furnace, and every heart
imbecile fingers thrumming on the windows
and fear lances every face, like a boil.

In all the stations all the carriages had been set on fire
I saw convoys of 60 engines racing at top speed, the horizon in heat
     pursuing, and flocks of crows flying after
disappearing
in the direction of Port Arthur

At Chita we had a few days respite
a break of five days, 'something on the line'
we stayed with Mr. Iankelevitch who wanted Flint to marry his only
     daughter
then the train set off again
now he'd taken over at the piano and he had toothache
and I daresay he can look back on the father's shop and the eyes of the
     girl who spent every night in his bed
and the afternoons in mine.
Mussorgsky
Hugo Wolf lieder
and the Gobi sands

And at Khailar there was a caravan of white camels
I think I was seeing pink elephants for about 500 km
but Flint was at the piano and he saw them too
you've got to close your eyes on a trip
and sleep
I was desperate for a kip
I recognised all the places with my eyes closed, by their smell
and learned to tell the trains by their rhythm
European trains keep common measure, and Asian ones quintuple or
      septuple time some, pianissimo, are lullabies
and there are some whose monotonous wheels remind me of the heavy
      prose of Marie Corelli
I decoded all the muddled messages of the wheels and rearranged the
      fragments into a terrible beauty
which I own
which pricks me on.

Qiqihar and Harbin
I'm not going further
It's the end of the line.
I got off at Harbin as the Red Cross offices were put to the torch.

O Paris
Great glowing hearth with streets crossing like charred sticks and old
      houses huddled over them for warmth
like a bunch of old grannies
And here are posters, read and green—all the colours, like my little
      yellow life
yellow, the lofty colour of French novels, like innocents, abroad.

Flint says he likes rubbing up against great cities on the bus and on foot
he's a pervert for cities
we take the Saint Germaine-Monmartre line to lay siege to the old Butte
the motor-cars bawl like golden bulls
the cows of twilight graze on the Sacré-Coeur

O Paris
Central disembarkation station for desires, junction of disquiet
only the druggists who sell paint still have a little light above their doors
and Flint is absorbed in the International Pullman and Great European
       Express Company brochure
rapt, he says 'It's the loveliest church in the world!'

I have friends that I can lean on like banisters
but they don't think of me when I'm not there
all the people I've ever known range themselves on the horizon
with gestures I can't make out and blurred faces, semaphoring something
       under the rain
Claire, Rob, Felicity, Nicola, Priya, Jonathan, and one or two more
the raffish lover I still hope to meet
when finally I come into possession of my proper body
oh, how that lonesome whistle blows
so many places racked with birthpangs
but China maybe isn't one of them right now

I wish I'd never gone anywhere
Tonight a fatal passion torments me
and despite myself I think of little Flint of the Ronson
over many lonely nights I wrote this poem in his honour
Flint
the little bit of rent
I'm sad so sad
I'll go to that plastic Paddy joint to remember my lost youth again
get a few pints in
and go home alone
like every other old roué

Paris

City of the Only Tower, the Gallows High, and the Wheel

Notes

Bülbülüm altın kafeste

A traditional Turkish song. The title means 'Nightingale in a golden cage'.

Poem beginning with a line by Patrick Califia

The line in question is from *Public Sex: The Culture of Radical Sex* (1994).

Splice

foid far ndís innocht, & / téit léignid becc etraib co ná dernaid aneaspa

From the 9th century Irish *Comrac Liadaine ocus Cuirithir*. The lovers Liadan and Curithir are instructed by their spiritual director to sleep together: 'Sleep by each other to-night!' said Cummine, 'And let a little scholar go between you lest you do any folly.'

Dycun, slepe sicury quile we wake, / and drede nouzt quile we lyve sestow.

The author of the (hostile) Kenilworth chronicle records these words, allegedly addressed to Richard II by one of his Cheshire Guardsmen, to demonstrate their notorious familiarity with the King. In modern English: 'Dickon, sleep soundly while we keep watch, and fear nothing while we're beside you.'

on the warren, in the lee of the firs

The title is a quotation from Mary Renault's novel *The Charioteer* (1953).

tardy steps her silent main

Howard Gardiner's statuette 'Lady on the Rocks' or 'White Lady' is a popular ornament found in many Irish homes. The fibre-glass cast of Gardiner's original clay model, which allowed for its mass reproduction, was made in the mid-1990s by Edward Loughman, who then sold the cast to Dublin Mouldings. His words are quoted from Jessie Ward's 2010 short documentary about the figurine.

Hero

'replie, you are deceaved, I am no woman/I':
from Christopher Marlowe, *Hero and Leander.*

IOU | OUI

Text loosely inspired by 'Hymn to Kali' (1922), a translation by Arthur
Avalon (Sir John Woodroffe) of a Sanskrit hymn, the *Karpūrādi-stotra.*

Pros of the Transsiberian & little Flint of the Ronson

Prose du Transsibérien et de la petite Jeanne de France, Blaise Cendrars'
hallucinatory account of a railway journey from Moscow to Harbin,
set against the violent backdrop of the Russo-Japanese war, was written
in 1913 in collaboration with the artist Sonia Delaunay and produced
as a limited-edition artist's book. Since then it has been translated into
English many times. With this version, I've tried to do something
slightly different: to represent Cendrars' tale from the point of view of
his 'companion', Jeanne (or Jehanne, as the name is spelled in the first
edition). Jeanne is a part of Cendrars' own consciousness, so some of this
re-imagining stays fairly close to the original. But in places the points
change, the narratives diverge and then re-encounter one another.

www.ingramcontent.com/pod-product-compliance
Lightning Source LLC
Chambersburg PA
CBHW031934080426
42734CB00007B/677